EXTREME WEATHER

HEAT WAVES AND DROUGHTS

Liza N. Burby

The Rosen Publishing Group's
PowerKids Press™
New York

Published in 1999 by The Rosen Publishing Group, Inc.
29 East 21st Street, New York, NY 10010

First Edition

Book Design: Resa Listort

Photo Credits: p. 4 © Skjold Photographs; pp. 6–7 © Chris Michaels/FPG International; p. 8 © Galen Rowell/Corbis; pp. 10–11 © Fidia Lisnawati/AP/Wide World; p. 12 © Telegraph Colour Library/FPG International; pp. 14–15 © Tom Nebbia/Corbis; p. 16 © Richard Gaul/FPG International; pp. 19, 20 © UPI/Corbis.

Burby, Liza N.
    Heatwaves and droughts / by Liza N. Burby.
        p. cm. — (Extreme weather)
    Includes index.
    Summary: Explains what heat waves and droughts are, where and when they happen, and what their effects can be.
    ISBN 0-8239-5292-4
    1. Heat waves (Meteorology)—Juvenile literature. 2. Droughts—Juvenile literature. [1. Heat waves (Meteorology).
    2. Droughts. 3. Weather.] I. Title. II. Series: Burby, Liza N. Extreme weather.
    QC981.8.B87 1998
    551.5'25—dc21   98-19930
    551.577   CIP
                                          AC r98

Manufactured in the United States of America

Contents

What Is a Heat Wave?

You may be happy during the first few days of warm weather. Sunny skies can mean lots of outdoor play. But when this weather drags on for days, and it gets hotter and stickier, you may feel uncomfortable. You may even wish for rain, since rain would help lower the hot **temperatures** (TEMP-rah-cherz). But there may be no sign of rain. And even the breeze feels hot.

This kind of hot weather can go on for weeks. When hot temperatures continue without getting cooler, it is called a heat wave.

◀ Warm weather can mean wearing summer clothes and playing outside with your friends.

What Is a Drought?

If sunny skies and hot temperatures continue for a week or more, the sun dries up all the **moisture** (MOYS-cher) in the ground, and the land can become scorched by the sun. As time passes without rain, soil becomes so thirsty and dry it turns crumbly. Water supplies may start to **evaporate** (ee-VAP-er-ayt). People may be asked to **conserve** (kun-SERV) water by not watering their lawns. Grass may turn brown as it bakes in the sun. Soon streams, lakes, and rivers can dry to a trickle. When an area doesn't get its usual rainfall for a long time, there is a **drought** (DROWT).

During times of drought, entire lakes can dry up. This sun-baked area was once a lake. ▶

When and Where Do They Happen?

Heat waves and droughts can happen anywhere in the world. A heat wave usually occurs during the summer months and may last only a few days. A drought can happen any time of the year and last for weeks, months, or even years. If a country or state gets less rain than it needs for plants to stay alive, there will be a drought. For example, the midwestern United States needs only 30 inches of rain per year to keep its plants alive. If this area gets only half the rainfall it needs, a drought will occur.

The amount of rainfall in an area is often measured to find out how much rain that area has received.

How Do They Start?

A heat wave is caused by a high **pressure** (PREH-sher) air **mass** (MASS). This air mass will stay in one place or move very slowly over an area. This causes the area beneath that air mass to heat up. It's almost like being stuck under a hot blanket.

No one understands exactly why a drought occurs. A drought doesn't always mean there hasn't been any rain. Rain is part of a water **cycle** (SY-kul) in which water evaporates and rises into the clouds. When the clouds become heavy with moisture, it rains. If rain clouds get blown away by wind or if an air mass keeps the clouds away, an area that needs rain may not get it.

When dried up by drought, bodies of water such as this pond in Indonesia can turn into walkways.

11

Heat Waves Can Be Dangerous

A heat wave can be dangerous in many ways. If animals or people get overheated, they can get sick from **heat stroke** (HEET STROHK). A person with heat stroke is no longer able to sweat, which is how a body cools itself. Without sweating, the body temperature can rise to dangerous levels. A person or animal with heat stroke should see a doctor right away. The sun can also damage our skin and cause bad sunburns.

Doctors tell people to stay indoors when it's very hot and try to stay cool by drinking cold liquids. During a heat wave, farmers worry that they will have no water for their crops or their **livestock** (LYV-stok). People who live near forests worry too. Twigs, leaves, or grass can become so dry that just a spark near these things can start a fire. Many forest fires start during heat waves.

Dangerous brush fires, such as this one in Australia, can be a result of heat waves.

Drought Can Be Harmful

Droughts can also be very dangerous. A drought can hurt the **environment** (en-VY-roh-ment). Animals, fish, and birds will die without water. Soil that is good for growing crops can become so dry it blows away. This is called **erosion** (ee-ROH-zhun). Erosion makes it harder to grow crops even when it does rain. And when crops die, people lose food. In some countries, droughts can cause problems for many years. If people are without food, a **famine** (FA-min) will occur. This has happened many times in very hot places such as Africa and India.

Both animals and people can suffer from a drought in desert areas where there is not much water to begin with. ▶

Preventing Drought

Earth has plenty of water. But the trick is to get the water to where people need it. Scientists have tried many ways to do this. One way is by cloud seeding. In cloud seeding, **chemicals** (KEH-mih-kulz) are dropped from airplanes into clouds. The chemicals are supposed to make rain in the clouds. But this doesn't always work. One way to get water to farms and other places is through **irrigation** (ih-rih-GAY-shun). Water is pulled from rivers through ditches or pipes to where it is needed. We also use groundwater, or water which is under the earth's surface. Groundwater is used when people dig **wells** (WELLZ). All of these ways can **prevent** (pre-VENT) drought.

Irrigation helps land, such as these bean fields, to get the water it needs.

Heat Waves and Drought in History

Drought has always been a problem for people. In 1988, the Midwest suffered from the worst drought in 50 years. It began with a dry winter and continued all summer. Temperatures got as high as 110 degrees. More than 5,000 people died. Heat waves, too, have caused problems. In the summer of 1994, there was a record heat wave across Europe. It was so hot in eastern Europe that train tracks became soft from the intense heat and bent in half! A heat wave in 1995 caused more than 1,000 deaths in the Midwest and on the East Coast of the United States.

Drought has caused problems throughout history. A drought in Little Rock, Arkansas, in 1934 caused this lake to dry up. As a joke, a sign was put up advertising land for sale where the lake used to be! ▶

The Dustbowl

One of the most famous droughts in history is the Great Drought, or the Dustbowl. From 1934 to 1941, very little rain fell on the Great Plains states of Colorado, Kansas, Nebraska, Oklahoma, and Texas. The weather was hot and dry. Crops, bushes, trees, and grass turned brown and died. Rivers and streams dried up. Many animals died.

Then the dry soil blew into the air in great clouds of dust, giving the area its name. Winds carried the dust everywhere, even through people's closed doors and windows, and all the way to the East Coast. When it was over, 50 million acres of farmland were ruined.

The Dustbowl of the 1930s affected over half of the United States of America.

Heat Waves, Drought, and the Future

Many scientists believe that the air around our planet is becoming hotter. This hot air is changing our **climate** (KLY-mit). This is called global warming. It will cause some parts of the world to be hotter and drier, and other parts to be cooler and wetter. Scientists are carefully watching the weather. They will tell people what is happening and how it will affect us. While heat waves are likely to bother us each summer, hopefully scientists will find more ways to protect people and crops if a drought happens.

Glossary

chemical (KEH-mih-kul) A substance that is used to cause a reaction.

climate (KLY-mit) The weather conditions of a certain place.

conserve (kun-SERV) To keep something from being wasted.

cycle (SY-kul) A series of events that repeats itself over and over.

drought (DROWT) A long period of dry weather with little or no rain.

environment (en-VY-roh-ment) All the living things and conditions that surround us.

erosion (ee-ROH-zhun) To be worn away slowly by wind or water.

evaporate (ee-VAP-er-ayt) When a liquid changes to a gas.

famine (FA-min) A shortage of food that causes people to starve.

heat stroke (HEET STROHK) An illness due to overheating of the body that includes the inability to sweat and a dangerously high body temperature.

irrigation (ih-rih-GAY-shun) To carry water to land through ditches or pipes.

livestock (LYV-stok) Farm animals.

mass (MASS) The amount of matter in something.

moisture (MOYS-cher) Water that is in the air or on the ground.

pressure (PREH-sher) A force put on something.

prevent (pre-VENT) To keep from happening.

temperature (TEMP-rah-cher) How hot or cold something is.

well (WELL) A hole dug in the ground for water.

Index